DREAM

DREAM

10 Minutes a Night and Turn Out the Light

CHER KAUFMANN

The Countryman Press
A division of W. W. Norton & Company
Independent Publishers Since 1923

For information about permission to reproduce selections from
this book, write to Permissions, The Countryman Press,
500 Fifth Avenue, New York, NY 10110

For information about special discounts for bulk purchases,
please contact W. W. Norton Special Sales at
specialsales@wwnorton.com or 800-233-4830

The Countryman Press
www.countrymanpress.com

A division of W. W. Norton & Company
500 Fifth Avenue, New York, NY 10110
www.wwnorton.com

978-1-58157-468-5 (pbk.)

1 2 3 4 5 6 7 8 9 0

To Sedona, who dreams awake

INTRODUCTION

The sweet and soothing lull of sleep opens the door and welcomes you to the world only seen behind resting eyelids. To dream, for many, is the brain's way of processing thoughts, bent from the kinks of the day, and to unravel those tight knots to a smooth creative thread, intertwining your waking and resting hours. Dreams can be filled with mystery and meaning; other times, they are a jumble of a funny joke and a trip to the park. And yet, to dream—the ability to move into possibility with infinite outcomes and limitlessness—can teach you who you really are.

Leonardo da Vinci once posed, "Why does the eye see a thing more clearly in dreams than the imagination when awake?" Perhaps if the same unrestricted vision were used in wakefulness as in dreams, there might be the same vibrancy and boundless potential in human connections. While we explore the vast gifts of dreams and muse on their mysteries, I invite you to release your day and extra thoughts for a few moments in order to suspend limitations and play in the infinite. Let's Dream.

How to use this book

- You may find the book helpful to read at your leisure in small, 10-minute blocks. You may reflect and contemplate the important messages any time.
- You can find calm by coloring the pages provided that are paired with passages and inspirational quotes. Use this activity as a relaxing coloring meditation.
- There are a dozen lined pages with "dream prompts" for jotting down special memories and ideas.
- Blank pages also contain simple drawing prompts for your moments of artistic creativity.
- Randomly open to a page to see what inspiration you might gain on a given day.

*"Who looks outside, dreams;
who looks inside, awakens."*

—Carl Jung

If your mind is dancing, slow it down by tuning into the lyrics and jotting down what comes to mind. Then remind yourself that it's time to sleep and rest; tomorrow you'll rise refreshed and ready to move mountains, if need be.

THE Moon WON'T USE THE DOOR, Only THE Window.
-RUMI

10-Minute Meditation

Slow Motion

Our mind is often what keeps us up at night. Train it to relax with this visualization.

Rest your head upon your pillow. Imagine being in a slow-motion scene from a movie. Your hair ribbons away from your face from a gentle breeze. Slow your breath to a deep, steady pace. Imagine your fingertips feel the very tippy tops of the grass blades as they wave in a feathery sea rolling with the whispering wind. Your skin feels the soft caress of the airstream as it curls around your arms, brushing off tension and releasing your shoulders from any weight they hold. Imagine relaxing on your back, looking up at the sky, allowing your arms and legs to feel heavy. The air softly whispers *hush* as it washes through the grass. You are fully supported by the earth. Let your body feel heavy. Relax a little more. In this slow-motion space, feel the corners of your mouth leisurely draw upward in a dreamy smile. Your eyes are closed now, and you can relax further, deeper in this slow-motion world.

"Silence is the sleep that nourishes wisdom."

—Francis Bacon

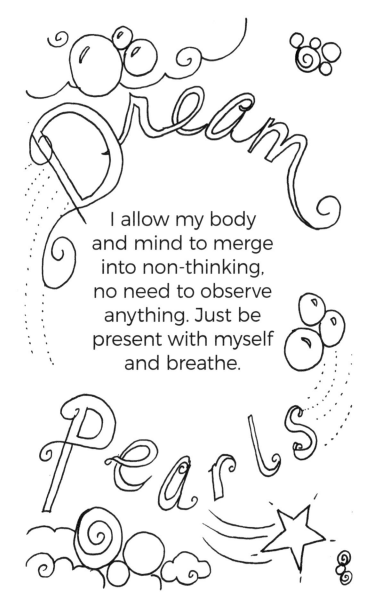

Dream

I allow my body
and mind to merge
into non-thinking,
no need to observe
anything. Just be
present with myself
and breathe.

Pearls

My Favorite Dreamy Words

Dream Journal

Dreams can speak to you through a language of pictures, sounds, places, people, and symbols. Dream journals can be done many ways. The most common is to write down as much as you can remember from the dream in a journal immediately upon waking. Keep the journal beside your bed so you can record in it at a moment's notice. Let your writings reflect what works best for you on this particular day. Draw a picture, write the scene in paragraph form, or put the most important words down on paper.

The second way to use a dream journal is to set an intention *before* going to sleep. Write your intention on top of the page in your dream journal and place it nearby before turning out the light. Once you are comfortably settled in bed with the lights out, hold the thought of your intention in your mind and allow it to be the last thing you think about before drifting off. Upon waking, record any dreams you had (even if it seems unrelated to your intention).

Notice if your dreams change between the two different ways of dream journaling.

I Dwell in Possibility

—Emily Dickinson—

"It is a common experience that a problem difficult at night is resolved in the morning after the committee of sleep has worked on it."

—John Steinbeck

EMBELLISH

Create Your Own Designs

ADD · ON

As a dreamer, an artist of all possibilities,
doodle a fabulous dreamy night scene with stars,
and perhaps stardust or a moon. It's your creation—
make it as magical as you want!

Listen to the Wind

Dreams often come in Soft Whispers

"A well spent day brings happy sleep."

—Leonardo da Vinci

10-Minute Meditation

Winding Down

One of the most soothing ways to get ready for sleep is to create a relaxing routine. Creating a routine not only signals to your body that you're winding down, it also sends messages of comfort and self-care as you move through the routine. Whatever your routine, it should include turning off all electronic devices 30 to 60 minutes minimum before going to bed.

Once you've had a chance to rest from looking at a screen, you will be ready to settle down. I like to add a calming scent to the air. Run an essential oil diffuser with a few drops of lavender. Clear your mind by coloring, reading, drawing, or meditating.

Just before you get under the covers, give yourself a short and gentle foot massage. Then your head: Run your fingers over your scalp in slow circles.

Make your routine simple and easy to follow. Be consistent and you will notice your body begin to respond to the first step in anticipation of relaxing. Try it for three days and you will see a difference.

"One of the most adventurous things left us is to go to bed. For no one can lay a hand on our dreams."

—E. V. Lucas

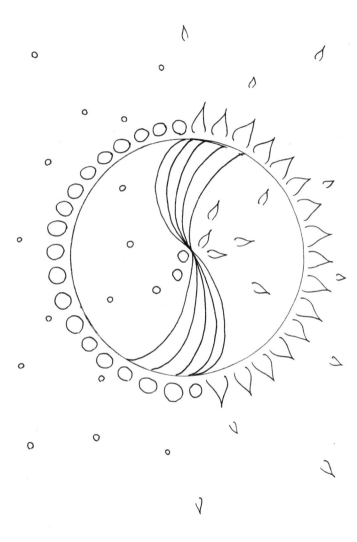

Where's your ideal comfy place to rest
(hammock, bed, tent, under the stars . . .)

All HUMAN BEINGS ARE ALSO *Dream Beings.* Dreaming ties All MANKIND TOGETHER.

—JACK KEROUAC

"Trust in dreams, for in them is hidden the gate to eternity."

—Khalil Gibran

Let go of ideas and thoughts that are weighing you down. Draw those feelings—in colors, shapes, words, whatever—floating off and out of your life.

DETACHMENT AND ENLIGHTENMENT

In many cultures there is an idea of connecting the personal and the communal to the point of oneness. In these teachings there is a subtle letting go, a detachment, if you will, from the concrete and absoluteness of what is seen or assumed. In the letting go of that which has always been known, the experience of what you now know grows, expands, and rises above to a new lookout point.

To become enlightened, in these teachings, is to release the gravity of attachments. When dreaming, you release doubts and past experiences that limit forward motion. Imagine the possibilities that could emerge if you practiced releasing ideas and thoughts that felt heavy to the mind, body, and heart. Be aware of what feeds the thoughts and feelings that create lightness and freedom.

This is the heart's desire—to be safe, to love and be loved, to be joyful, and to be at one with personal purpose and freedom of expression.

"Now I see the secret of making the best person: it is to grow in the open air and to eat and sleep with the earth."

—Walt Whitman

What You Seek is Seeking You

-RUMI

10-Minute Meditation

Moon Meditation

In the light of the moon if possible, or at least in your imagination, sit in a comfortable position cross-legged on the floor or upright in a chair with your feet flat touching the earth. Sit up straight and tall. Relax your hands.

Take a deep breath, allowing your shoulders to rise ever so slightly and naturally on the inhale, then soften your shoulders, let them drop down and roll your shoulder blades closer together on the exhale. This will create a natural expansion of your chest and open the area of the heart.

From this place of quietness, just breathe. Naturally, inward, outward. Feel the crown of your head open to the light of the moon. It might feel tingly or cool. Imagine the rays of the moon washing away any extra energy from the day. Feel your skin lighten as it breathes. Can you feel excess heat move away from your body as it receives moonlight?

Now, on your next inhale, breathe in the moon. Breathe in the coolness of the light—maybe you feel your head turn upward slightly, maybe your jaw softens.

The moon whispers wisdom and provides light when it is dark. The cosmic glow lights up your cells, feeds them, assists in growth. Feel the soft wave, a gentle hush that moves between your body and the moon. This rhythm of moon and body is life in quietude.

Breathe in the moonlight, let it swirl within you, and then breathe out the moonlight. Allow this moment to linger.

Do you consider yourself an early bird or a night owl?

What is your favorite dream flavor? Using the word "dream," draw something you'd like to eat (Swooshbloom Dream Pie, Savory Dream Rice Fluff, Cotton Candy Dream Cloud, Dreamberry Licorice . . .)

Take a Trip in my Airship

In 1904, George "Honey Boy" Evans and Ren Shields wrote an imaginative song about a traveler who would pick up his beloved to sail through the night on an airship, flying past Venus and Mars and stopping for a visit with the man in the moon.

The sweet song of love includes the lure of fantasy and whimsy that we often forget to visit within our imaginations. There are times when we all benefit from the deep fantasy of dreams without limits, a chance to visualize without doubts or shoulds. In this place, we allow our body, mind, and spirit to unlock from an anchored rock of perceived reality and be free and light.

When we let go of absolutes, our subconscious creative mind can often connect with out-of-the-box solutions, concepts, and notions of fancy. When we trust our creative ideas, we alter our reality to meet us with flexibility in making a world of happiness and glee.

"You're made of star stuff."

—Carl Sagan

10-Minute Meditation

Massage

Acupuncture utilizes different points on the body to open up energy flow for the mind, body, and spirit, and it offers functional, sustainable longevity. Often these points are grouped in categories of function or in support of an organ. The organs each represent unique physical, emotional, and spiritual connections. A single point in acupuncture connects to the organs. An acupuncture needle triggers support to various areas of the body, mind, and spirit. One group of points is called "Window to the Sky."

These points have physical purposes that connect the physical brain to the physical body. But there is a deeper, more substantial purpose to these points. They also open creativity and connection to the spirituality of the life within the body, mind, and spirit as a whole glorious unit. Imagine living from a place where your physical and spiritual parts could relax, sleep, or dream with a window open to the sky, an open skylight connecting you to your highest potential, channeling through your whole being to reside within you.

A relaxing neck massage can help to open the windows to the sky, the brain to the body, and all potential to your inner being.

Curve your left fingers into the top muscles of your right shoulder and rub in small firm circles. Do this especially on the sore spots. Repeat with the right hand on the left shoulder. Then place your left fingers along the left side of your spine at the back of your neck (not on the spine, but next to it) with the base of your palm on the side of your neck, and do the same on the right side with your right hand. Apply gentle pressure with your fingers and palms in a slow squeezing or kneading motion. Last, gently tug on your earlobes several times downward and then outward. Massage the whole outside of your ear, with a gentle circular tugging between your thumb and fingers, going all around the rim. If you ever feel dizzy, press on your breast bone (sternum) and take a few slow, deep breaths.

"The interpretation of dreams is the royal road to a knowledge of the unconscious activities of the mind."

—Sigmund Freud

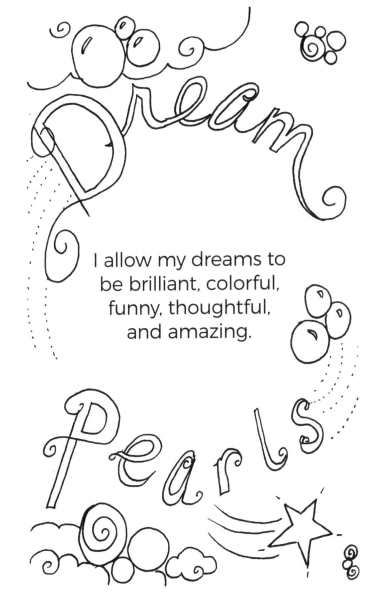

I allow my dreams to
be brilliant, colorful,
funny, thoughtful,
and amazing.

Do You See This as DAY or NIGHT?

Add more clouds or stars and color.

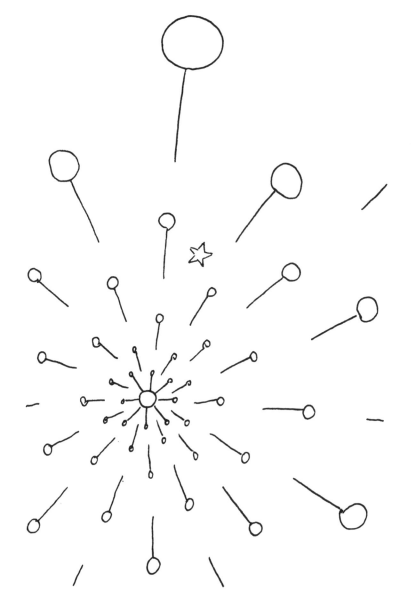

"*Think in the morning. Act in the noon. Eat in the evening. Sleep in the night.*"

—William Blake

The Journey OF A THOUSAND Miles BEGINS BENEATH one's FEET

— LAO TZU

Sleep to Dream, Sleep to Heal

Sleep has such a wonderful way of lulling the body and mind into deeper stages, like a breath, rising and falling, expanding and releasing. A symphony of gradual change that allows the body and the mind to process, heal, and reset.

The stages of slumber gradually and gently move you through the drapery of wakefulness, softly rustling behind you and guiding you into a vast space beyond doors or walls to infinite possibilities within the sleep architecture. Each stage of slumber slides more deeply in rhythm than the previous stage, only to emerge slightly to repeat the slow dance again and again throughout the night. The mind and body inhale and exhale, creating and molding a new mind and body.

Traditional Chinese Medicine and Ayurveda suggest that the most beneficial sleep happens when the body is resting by 11 p.m. each night. Your organs need time to do their job in harmony with all the biorhythms of your being. Allow your body to rejuvenate. Resting places are healing places.

Rain can be soft, soothing as it brings life and awakens all it touches. It is also proof that nature has a voice that sings, howls as well as thunders. What do you think of when you think of the word *rain*?

"At night, I open the window and ask the moon to come and press its face against mine."

—Rumi

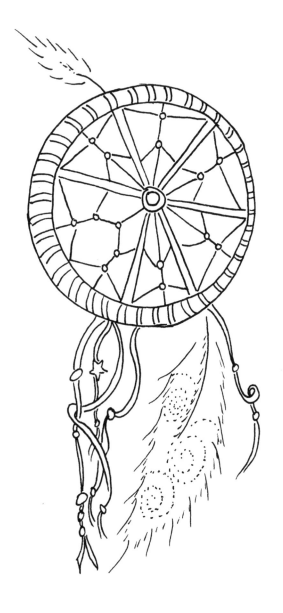

"Forget not that the earth delights to feel your bare feet and the winds long to play with your hair."

—Khalil Gibran

EARTHLY PLEASURES, FANTASY DREAMS

Symbolism in dreams, in poetry, and in art must contain something familiar in order to bridge a deeper meaning. People, places, and experiences that make an impression upon us are captured through our emotions, behaviors, and memories. Your cells are created from the food they are given in all forms, including what you feed them symbolically. When you feed your emotions and mind with uplifting and beneficial experiences, you lock in an intention of purpose and nourishment to your being.

Being aware of the creativity in nature—the colors, sounds, and textures—and appreciating the "as-is-ness" of the spectrum around you both connect you to the beauty and possibility of knowing more. Movies, books, and art contain magical descriptions and images to heighten your visual and emotional outlook based upon real-life experiences. The ebbs and tides of long grass in a gentle breeze or the salty breath of the ocean whispering in your ear can be absorbed into a greater expression of you as your creative awareness moves into your fantasies and dreams.

You are not a drop in the Ocean. You are the Entire Ocean in A DROP

-RUMI

"A good laugh and a long sleep are the best cures in the doctor's book."

—Irish Proverb

THE MIND THAT OPENS TO A NEW IDEA NEVER RETURNS TO ITS ORIGINAL SIZE

-Albert Einstein-

Draw Your Own Fluffy Sheep

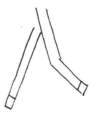

Counting Blessings

Counting sheep has long been suggested as a means of distraction to enter sleep. *Disciplina Clericalis,* written in the early twelfth century by Petrus Alphonsi, shares a story about a king who requested additional stories from his nightly storyteller. The storyteller speaks to the king of a farmer who purchases two thousand sheep but, upon reaching the river, the farmer must transport the sheep across two at a time. The storyteller falls asleep and the king awakens him, insisting that he finish the story. The storyteller says the farmer needs time to move all the sheep and the king must keep track of the sheep as they cross. In *Don Quixote*, Sancho asks Don Quixote to keep track of the goats as they cross a river or else the story ends. However, studies suggest that this kind of distraction leads to a busy mind rather than a relaxed one. Next time, count your blessings rather than sheep. Feelings of gratitude and love soften the mind, open the heart, and relax the body. Visualizing a tranquil location or favorite place has proven to be more beneficial in inducing a sense of fulfillment and relaxation. Feel the air, the temperature, and the colors of what brings you peacefulness. Where is your favorite place? What are your blessings?

Draw the moons you see in your dreams.

LOOK at the **moon** in the **SKY**, **NOT** the one in the **Lake**.

— RUMI

*"Dreams are the touchstones
of our character."*

—Henry David Thoreau

Dream

I say "Thank you" and "I love you" to my mind and body for all they do each day. Now is the time to rest and it is OK to relax.

Pearls